For:

· ·

From:

· ·

Date:

· ·

© 2012 by Barbour Publishing, Inc.

ISBN 978-1-61626-412-3

Written and compiled by Janice Hanna Thompson.

Published by Barbour Publishing, Inc., P.O. Box 719, Uhrichsville, Ohio 44683, www.barbourbooks.com

Our mission is to publish and distribute inspirational products offering exceptional value and biblical encouragement to the masses.

Member of the
Evangelical Christian
Publishers Association

Printed in China.

Fabulosity

365 Fabulous Thoughts
for Women

BARBOUR
PUBLISHING

Day 1

. . . .

You Are a Masterpiece

Sure, God created man before woman.
But then you always make a rough
draft before the final masterpiece.

UNKNOWN

Day 2
· · · · · · ·
A Little Confidence Goes a Long, Long Way

Want to be truly fabulous?
Exude confidence. There's nothing more
appealing than a bold, confident woman
who knows where she's going and has the
courage to take the right steps to get there.

Day 3
· · · · · · ·
Fabulous Is as Fabulous Does

Many women think they're fabulous
because of the way they look or the
perfume they wear. The real test of
fabulosity is on the inside. If you're truly
fabulous, you will be kindhearted and
generous. Your actions will be a
reflection of your heart.

Day 4

. . . .

The Girly Girl

Some of us are just born girly girls.
We're into hair, makeup, shoes,
and all of the other frills that come
along with the territory. The best part
of being a girly girl?
Having compassion and kindness
toward those who are not!

Day 5

• • • • • • •

Twice as Well

Whatever women must do,
they must do twice as well as
men to be thought half as good.
Luckily, this is not difficult.

CHARLOTTE WHITTON

Day 6

. . . .

Makeup. . .

Ever been through a breakup in a
friendship? Maybe there's a certain
girlfriend you haven't spoken to in ages.
Today, reach into your "makeup" bag.
Do what you can to mend the relationship.
Dig deep. . .and make things
fabulous once again.

Day 7

· · · · · · · ·

What's in Your Purse?

Purses are, in and of themselves, fabulous.
What you carry in them says a lot about
who you are and where your interests lie.
Take a peek inside your purse. Are you
hanging on to things you should let go of?

Day 8
· · · · · · · ·
Someday My Prince Will Come

Ah, Prince Charming! How we delight
in the idea of finding him. He'll come
sweeping in on a white horse and save the
day. Okay, so maybe the fairy tale isn't
exactly real. . .but that doesn't mean you
won't find your prince. If you haven't
already met your Prince Charming,
just hang on. Could be he's already got
a castle prepared. . .just for you!

Day 9
· · · · · · · ·
Date Night

There's nothing more fabulous than sharing a date night with the man you love. Getting away from the hustle and bustle of work, the kids, the bills. . .just the two of you, tucked away at a corner table in a restaurant or sneaking kisses in the back row of the theater.

Day 10
· · · · · · · ·
Those Fab High Heels!

High heels were invented by a woman
who had been kissed on the forehead.

CHRISTOPHER MORLEY

Day 11
. . . .
A Fabulous Heart

Women have great hearts. They care
about their children, their spouses, friends,
coworkers, and many more people, besides.
Above everything you could own in this
world, strive to have a truly fabulous heart.

Day 12

Keep Those Fabulous
Friendships Alive

A friendship can weather most things
and thrive in thin soil; but it needs a
little mulch of letters and phone calls
and small, silly presents every so
often—just to save it from
drying out completely.

PAM BROWN

Day 13

. . . .

Beauty Sleep

Is there anything more wonderful than getting eight glorious hours of sleep? No interruptions. Nothing but eight blissful hours of z's! Talk about a fabulous beauty treatment!

Day 14

· · · · · · · · ·

What *Do* We Want?

If you were to poll a group of men, asking
the question, "What do women want?"
how do you suppose they would respond?
Even women struggle to know the answer.
Deep in our hearts, we all long to be loved,
accepted, and understood. Receiving all
three is truly fabulous!

Day 15

· · · · · · · ·

Classy Lady!

A girl should be two things:
classy and fabulous.

COCO CHANEL

Day 16
· · · · · · · · ·
Letting Yourself Go

It's one thing to let yourself go, physically.
It's another thing to "let go" of your fears,
your inhibitions, and your jealousies.
Today would be a terrific day to "let
yourself go" when it comes to the things
you shouldn't be hanging on to.

Day 17

· · · · · · · · ·

Relationships—You and Me!

Me without you is like a shoe without laces, a deck of cards without aces, asentencewithoutspaces.

UNKNOWN

Day 18

. . . .

Working Out

If you're having a rough day, working out can turn things around and make you feel fabulous, inside and out. You really can exercise your way to a better frame of mind—and get in shape while you're at it!

Day 19

Relaxed and Invigorated

Probably one of the greatest gifts you can give yourself is a one-hour massage with a really good masseuse. Whether you choose a Swedish massage with hot rocks or a deep tissue massage to soothe your aching muscles, you'll leave feeling relaxed and invigorated. Fabulous!

Day 20

Four Things

Four things a woman should know:
How to look like a girl; how to act
like a lady; how to think like a man;
and how to work like a dog.

UNKNOWN

Day 21

· · · · · · · ·

Makeover Madness

They're everywhere—those makeover TV
shows. Everything's being flipped—houses,
cars, rooms. . .even people! If you want
to live a truly fabulous life, you have to
occasionally be willing to undergo
a makeover. What area of your life needs
a makeover today?

Day 22

. . . .

The Stuff We Love

Oh, how we love our bling! Necklaces,
earrings, shoes, purses. You name it,
we love it! When it comes to the things
we value most in this life, however, the list
changes. We treasure our friends,
our family, our loved ones, and our faith.
Truly, there's no bling in the world
that even comes close.

Day 23

Clean House

Is there anything more wonderful to a woman than a spotless house? Some of us can only dream of such a miracle!
If you're feeling swallowed up by stuff, don't despair. Start small and work your way up to a fabulous, clean home.

Day 24

. . . .

Gossip Girls

Being "in the know" is a lot of fun, isn't it?
There's something so great about hanging
out with the girls and gabbing about
everything from our struggles to our
hopes and dreams. As long as we're
careful not to hurt others with our words,
girlish chatter can be quite fab!

Day 25
· · · · · · · · · ·

Let's Go Shopping!

When women are depressed,
they either eat or go shopping.
Men invade another country.

ELAYNE BOOSLER

Day 26

. . . .

Not-So-Desperate Housewives

A woman who has her head on straight knows there's more to being a housewife than caring for a house. And she doesn't see her situation as desperate, either. In fact, she rather enjoys who she is and what she does. There's something pretty fabulous about caring for home and family!

Day 27

. . . .

Happily-Ever-Afters

From the time we were little girls,
we dreamed of happily-ever-afters.
We want things to end well. As grown-up
girls, we realize that things don't always
turn out like we'd hoped.
However, we can—and should—
still have a positive, childlike attitude.
Good things are coming!

Day 28

A Hot Bath

There must be quite a few things
that a hot bath won't cure,
but I don't know many of them.

SYLVIA PLATH

Day 29

· · · · · · · · · ·

Keeping Your Cool

Don't you love women who know how to keep their cool, even when everyone— and everything—around them is at the boiling point? There's something pretty special about a woman who doesn't blow her top when situations spiral out of control!

Day 30

. . . .

Getting It Done

Put "eat chocolate" at the top of your
list of things to do today. That way,
at least you'll get one thing done.

UNKNOWN

Day 31
· · · · · · · · ·
Sister Time

Whether it's your sister, friend, mom,
Bible study group, or female coworkers,
"sister time" is a blast! And let's face it,
sister-friends are our best supporters,
sticking with us through thick and thin.
Who better to spend time with?

Day 32

· · · · · · · · · ·

Woman's Instinct

I would rather trust a woman's
instinct than a man's reason.

STANLEY BALDWIN

Day 33

. . . .

Connecting with an Old Friend

Don't you love it when you hear from
an old friend? Maybe she surprises you
with a call or an e-mail. Though months
(or even years) have passed, you laugh and
talk as though you've never been apart.
There's something to be said
for longevity, isn't there?

Day 34

· · · · · · · · ·

Great Bedding

Ooo-la-la! What luxury! What a taste of the high life! There's just something about great sheets, a great comforter, and luxurious pillows that can make a girl feel like a queen. Instead of checking into an expensive hotel, pick up some fabulous bedding and give your bedroom a makeover. You're sure to sleep like a baby.

Day 35
· · · · · · · · ·
Photo Op

The rarest thing in the world is a woman
who is pleased with photographs of herself.

ELIZABETH METCALF

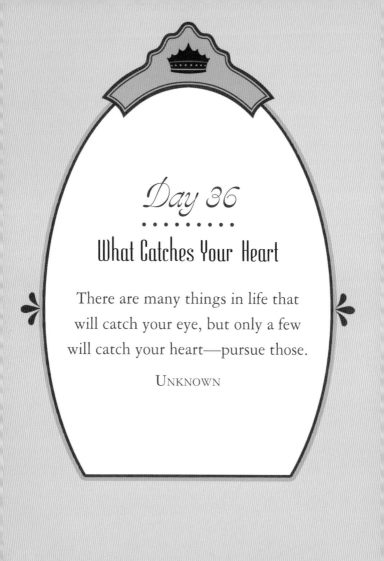

Day 36

. . . .

What Catches Your Heart

There are many things in life that
will catch your eye, but only a few
will catch your heart—pursue those.

UNKNOWN

Day 37

. . . .

I Am Woman!

I am woman!
I am invincible!
I am pooped!

UNKNOWN

Day 38

· · · · · · · · ·

A Good Cry

God knew what He was doing when He
gave us the ability to release our emotions
through our tears. Getting it all out can
be so cleansing, so healing. If you've been
holding it in, let it go! Those tears are a
fabulous gift, meant to bring sweet release.

Day 39

· · · · · · · · · ·

Every Woman's Dream

It's every woman's dream: Going into the
closet, selecting a dress, putting it on. . .
and discovering it's too big!
Is there anything more fun than finding
out you've dropped a whole dress size?
What a fabulous excuse to shop!

Day 40
· · · · · · · · · ·

Dieting Humor

I've been on a diet for two weeks,
and all I've lost is fourteen days.

TOTIE FIELDS

Day 41
· · · · · · · · ·
Unexpected Surprises

Every now and again, life surprises us
with something unexpected. A promotion
at work, for instance. Maybe you've been
working away at your job and wonder
if anyone's noticed. Hang on!
Your day is coming!

Day 42
· · · · · · · · · ·
Great Movies

Action-packed adventures.
Sappy romances. Dazzling dramas.
There's something about seeing a truly
fabulous movie, one that sweeps you away
to another time or place. A great movie can
change both your mood and your outlook.

Day 43

. . . .

Healthy Choices

Choosing to walk instead of taking the car. Choosing to take the stairs instead of the elevator. Going with the salad instead of the fried chicken. These are all healthy alternatives. Your body and mind will thank you for making fabulous choices.

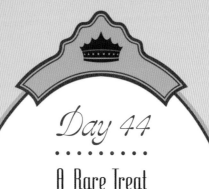

Day 44

· · · · · · · · · ·

A Rare Treat

Ah, "me" time! When you're caring
for a houseful of kiddos, getting time
to yourself is a rare treat. Some moms
lock themselves in the bathroom for a
few minutes of peace and quiet.
Don't worry, Mom. Those kids are
growing up fast. Pretty soon you'll
have more "me" time than you
know what to do with.

Day 45

· · · · · · · · · ·

Cinderella's Slipper

I like Cinderella, I really do. She has a good work ethic. I appreciate a good, hard-working gal. And she likes shoes. The fairy tale is all about the shoe at the end, and I'm a big shoe girl.

AMY ADAMS

Day 46

· · · · · · · · · ·

The First Day of Spring

Glorious! Colorful! Vibrant! These are all
words to describe the first day of spring.
Just yesterday, the ground was frozen
over. Now, miraculously, flowers peek
through with the promise of a new season.
Fabulous, fabulous spring!

Day 47
· · · · · · · · · ·
Older Women

There's something pretty amazing about
older women. They walked the road
before us and stood strong, in spite of life's
adversities. Today, tip your hat to a senior
woman. Tell her she's fabulous.

Day 48

Dancing Backwards

Remember, Ginger Rogers did
everything Fred Astaire did,
but backwards and in high heels.

Faith Whittlesey

Day 49

. . . .

A Night on the Town

Whether it's a night out with the girls,
date night with your husband or boyfriend,
or a fun night out with your kids,
there's something pretty fabulous about
getting out of the house and doing
something different. Grab those heels!
It's time for a night out on the town!

Day 50
· · · · · · · · ·
Why Women Exist

If women didn't exist, all the money
in the world would have no meaning.

UNKNOWN

Day 51

. . . .

Glamour

When you think of the word *glamour*
what comes to mind? Fashion models?
A fantastic makeup job? Runway shows?
The latest fashions from Paris?
The word *glamour* refers to people
who are appealing or attractive.
Want to be truly attractive to others?
Love them unconditionally.

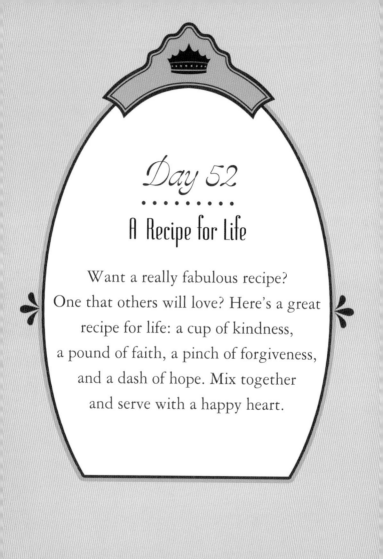

Day 52

. . . .

A Recipe for Life

Want a really fabulous recipe?
One that others will love? Here's a great
recipe for life: a cup of kindness,
a pound of faith, a pinch of forgiveness,
and a dash of hope. Mix together
and serve with a happy heart.

Day 53

. . . .

Girlfriends

Sometimes you've just got to spend time with your girlfriends. A boyfriend won't do. A husband won't do. A male coworker won't do. Many of life's rougher situations call for sister-friend time.

Day 54
. . . .
A Great Book

Don't you love those leisurely days
when you actually have the time to
settle in with a good book?
There's something rather fabulous about
being whisked away by a good story,
isn't there? A good book is more than an
escape. . .it's a place to dream, to hope,
and to discover new possibilities.

Day 55

. . . .

Chocolate Never Grows Old

Flowers wilt, jewelry tarnishes, and candles
burn out. . .but chocolate doesn't hang
around long enough to get old.

UNKNOWN

Day 56

. . . .

Concealer

All women love concealer. It hides a
multitude of things—blemishes, freckles,
and other imperfections. There's another
kind of concealer that's equally fabulous
(if not more so). It's called love. Love is the
perfect way to conceal—and heal!—
hurt, bitterness, or pain.

Day 57

. . . .

A Different Point of View

I long to accomplish a great and noble task, but it is my chief duty to accomplish small tasks as if they were great and noble.

HELEN KELLER

Day 58
. . . .
Definition of Success

Success is getting what you want;
happiness is wanting what you get.

INGRID BERGMAN

Day 59
. . . .
Verve

Verve is defined as energy and enthusiasm,
particularly as it relates to expressing ideas.
Why is verve such a fabulous thing to
women? We're all about expressing ideas,
and we tend to do so with great energy
and enthusiasm. Verve! Let it flow!

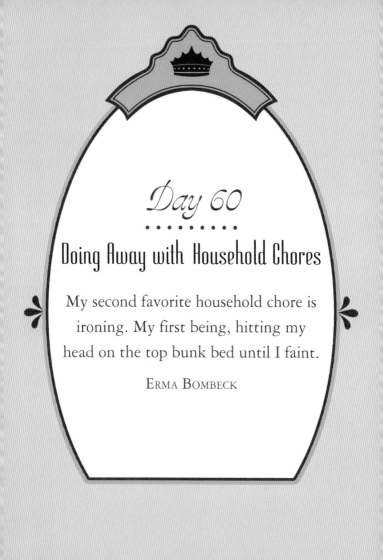

Day 60

· · · · · · · · · ·

Doing Away with Household Chores

My second favorite household chore is
ironing. My first being, hitting my
head on the top bunk bed until I faint.

ERMA BOMBECK

Day 61
. . . .
That Certain Spark

Have you ever met someone who has
"that certain spark"? Could be a child with
a creative spark. Might be a coworker with
a work ethic that sparks others to action.
Might be someone of the opposite sex who
sparks romantic thoughts each time you
look at him. Who knows. . .
it could even be you!

Day 62
· · · · · · · · · ·
Freshly Shaved Legs

Oh, the joy of freshly shaved legs!
Smooth as silk. No stubble. Ready to
face the world. Clean-shaven legs?
Truly fabulous.

Day 63

· · · · · · · · · ·

The Happy Dance

Ever feel so fabulous about life that you
want to do the happy dance?
Well, go right ahead! What's stopping you?
Dance is a celebration—an outward
expression of something joyous going on
inside your heart. Get to it! Move those feet!

Day 64
· · · · · · · · · ·
Still Standing

Have you ever met a woman so resilient,
so strong, that she remained standing after
life dealt her hard blows? What a fabulous
example of inner strength! Today, make up
your mind to be as resilient as that woman.
You can stand strong, even when the winds
of life threaten to blow you down.

Day 65
· · · · · · · · · ·
Sense of the Beautiful

A person should hear a little music,
read a little poetry, and see a fine picture
every day of their life, in order that worldly
cares may not obliterate the sense
of the beautiful which God has
implanted in the human soul.

JOHANN WOLFGANG VON GOETHE

Day 66
. . . .
Flower Power

Some of us are born with green thumbs.
Others have to work hard to keep flowers
alive. Still, there's nothing prettier than
a garden of flowers in full bloom.
Azaleas, daisies, roses. . .they're all
fabulous, alive with color and life.

Day 67

. . . .

The Long-Awaited First Kiss

Oh, the sense of anticipation! The wonder,
the anguish! "Will he kiss me, or won't
he?" Finally—after thinking it might never
happen—the kiss! That glorious, blissful,
knee-buckling first kiss! And boy,
was it ever worth the wait!

Day 68

. . . .

Happy Endings

I always wanted a happy ending. . . .
Now I've learned the hard way that
some poems don't rhyme, and some
stories don't have a clear beginning,
middle, and end. Life is about not
knowing, having to change, taking the
moment and making the best of
it without knowing what's going
to happen next.

GILDA RADNER

Day 69

. . . .

A Day at the Spa

Imagine you've got a full day at a local spa.
What will you do first? Get a massage?
A mani/pedi? A facial? No matter what
you choose, it's sure to be great.
Being pampered is a real luxury,
one we don't experience often enough.
Oh, but how fabulous when we do get
the spa treatment!

Day 70
· · · · · · · · · ·

Short People in the House

A woman knows all about her children.
She knows about dentist appointments,
soccer games, romances, best friends,
locations of friends' houses, favorite foods,
secret fears, and hopes and dreams.
A man is vaguely aware of some short
people living in the house.

UNKNOWN

Day 71

. . . .

Matching Socks

When we were children, we never thought
much about matching socks, did we?
Only as we age do we realize the value
of actually having two socks that match.
(And where are all of those missing socks,
anyway? Do you suppose there's a basket
waiting for us in heaven?)

Day 72

· · · · · · · · · ·

Perspective

I actually recall fixating on the fact that
my thighs a-l-m-o-s-t touched at the top. . . .
If I could go back in time and slap my
eighteen-year-old self, I would. I would tell
her to snap out of it, because that's the best
your thighs will ever be. You should take
pictures of your thighs right now so you
can remember how amazing they were!

ANITA RENFROE

Day 73

. . . .

Girls Just Wanna Have "Funds"

Most of us want to have our act together,
financially and otherwise. It's a wise
woman who discovers how to earn, handle,
and save money. What a fabulous present
we give ourselves when we figure out how
to manage money effectively!

Day 74

Do It Anyway

I was asked to act when I couldn't act.
I was asked to sing "Funny Face" when
I couldn't sing, and dance with Fred
Astaire when I couldn't dance—and do all
kinds of things I wasn't prepared for.
Then I tried like mad to cope with it.

AUDREY HEPBURN

Day 75

. . . .

Nice-Looking!

You want to fall in love with a shoe,
go ahead. A shoe can't love you back;
but, on the other hand, a shoe can't hurt
you too deeply either. And there are so
many nice-looking shoes.

ALLAN SHERMAN

Day 76

New Underwear

Ladies, you must admit. . .it feels awfully
good to toss those old panties and bras
and start fresh. There's something rather
exciting about a drawer full of new
"unmentionables" that makes one
want to mention it!

Day 77

An Expression of Beauty

The expression a woman wears on her face is more important than the clothes she wears on her back.

DALE CARNEGIE

Day 78

· · · · · · · · · ·

D. I. Y.

Doing it yourself can be a fabulous
alternative to paying an expert—
if your heart is in it and you've got the
know-how. What better way to say
"I am woman, hear me roar!" than with a
hammer in your hand?

Day 79

· · · · · · · · · ·

Enchanted

Women are so easily influenced—
by flattering words, dashing heroes,
and others who attempt to hoodwink us.
Today, make a fabulous personal choice
not to be taken in by those who are
calling your bluff. Stand firm.
Don't be hoodwinked!

Day 80
. . . .

Gains and Losses

I've been on a constant diet for the last
two decades. I've lost a total of 789
pounds. By all accounts, I should be
hanging from a charm bracelet.

ERMA BOMBECK

Day 81

. . . .

Calgon, Take Me Away!

Remember the old commercial for Calgon bath crystals? What better way to sneak away from life's woes than in a bubble bath? Great bath products don't just smell and feel fabulous, they really do whisk you away from your troubles (at least for an hour or so)!

Day 82
. . . .
Perfect Pedicure

Ah, the pedicure! It's the perfect solution
to a bad day. Where else can you get
clean feet, a foot and leg massage, and
pretty pink toenails, all in the same place?
Fabulous, darling. . .simply fabulous!

Day 83
. . . .
Snuggle Time!

Every mama knows that snuggling in bed
with the kids gathered around is a fabulous
feeling. Whether you're tickling, laughing,
telling stories, or reading a book,
there's no better way to pass the time.

Day 84

. . . .

Someone to Listen

Sometimes we just need a friend or loved one to sit with us while we're pouring our heart out. Doesn't it feel good to have someone listen. . .*really* listen?

Day 85

Older. . .or Younger?

The older theory was, marry an older
man because they're more mature.
But the new theory is men don't
mature. Marry a younger one.

RITA RUDNER

Day 86

· · · · · · · · · ·

Backup Plan

Successful women know the secret—
in order to succeed, you've got to have
a fabulous backup plan. When Plan A
falls through (and it often does),
you're ready to go with Plan B.
You're not discouraged or panicked.
You simply shift gears and keep going.

Day 87

· · · · · · · · · ·

Possibilities

At the height of laughter,
the universe is flung into a
kaleidoscope of new possibilities.

JEAN HOUSTON

Day 88
· · · · · · · · · ·
Chick Flicks

Grab the tissues and gather the girlfriends! It's chick-flick night! Truly, there's nothing more fabulous than hanging out with your friends at the movies, particularly the latest romantic comedy or drama. You can laugh together, cry together, and sigh together.

Day 89

. . . .

Working Together to Find a Cure

As women, we're all aware of the
devastation of breast cancer. Many of us
have friends or loved ones who've been
affected. That's why we need to band
together. Arm in arm, hand in hand,
we can make a difference as we work
together—truly together—to find a cure.
A cancer-free world. . .now,
wouldn't that be fabulous?

Day 90

· · · · · · · · · ·

Chocolate Cake

Inside some of us is a thin person struggling to get out, but they can usually be sedated with a few pieces of chocolate cake.

Unknown

Day 91
. . . .
Laughing with Someone You Love

Laughter is fabulous, no matter who you
share it with. Still, there's something pretty
amazing about laughing with someone
you love. You're sharing something much
deeper than a good joke or a funny reaction
to a situation. . .you're sharing from the
depth of your relationship.

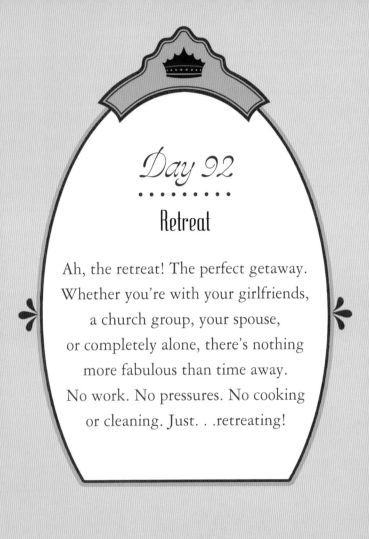

Day 92

. . . .

Retreat

Ah, the retreat! The perfect getaway.
Whether you're with your girlfriends,
a church group, your spouse,
or completely alone, there's nothing
more fabulous than time away.
No work. No pressures. No cooking
or cleaning. Just. . .retreating!

Day 93

. . . .

Silly Love Songs

You'd think that people would've had
enough of silly love songs. . .but they
haven't! There's something pretty fabulous
about those goofy lyrics, that sweet-as-pie
melody, and that singsongy feel.
Makes you feel like falling in love
all over again!

Day 94

· · · · · · · · · ·

Fabulous Choices

Choice is a gift given to everyone.
It is a powerful gift that can
change your life.

UNKNOWN

Day 95

Tossing the Masks

Women are great at wearing masks.
We pretend to be happy when we're not.
We put on the mask of comedy to cover
up pain. Sometimes the best mask you
can wear is your own face with real,
honest emotions etched into every crevice.
No masks. No pretense.
Just fabulous, fresh honesty.

Day 96

. . . .

Adorned Accordingly

Know, first, who you are;
and then adorn yourself accordingly.

EPICTETUS

Day 97

. . . .

Lemonade Makers

Some people don't do a very good job of
handling life's tragedies. They succumb
to the pressures and get defeated.
But not you! No, you turn lemons
into lemonade. In fact, you've learned
to love lemonade!

Day 98
· · · · · · · · · ·
Intuition

God made man stronger but not
necessarily more intelligent. He gave
women intuition and femininity. And, used
properly, that combination easily jumbles
the brain of any man I've ever met.

FARRAH FAWCETT

Day 99

. . . .

Sweet Kisses

Ah, kisses! Those mushy, romantic,
knees-turn-to-Jell-O kisses from the man
you love. They can lift your mood,
set your feet on the right path, and make
you believe all is right with the world,
even when things are tough.

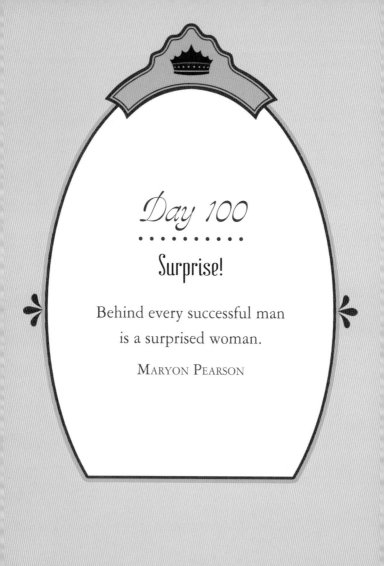

Day 100

· · · · · · · · · ·

Surprise!

Behind every successful man
is a surprised woman.

MARYON PEARSON

Day 101
· · · · · · · · · ·
Coffee and Conversation

While all women are not coffee fans,
most love great conversation. What better
place than at a coffee shop, or seated across
the breakfast table from a good friend?
There's something fabulous about the
combination of coffee and conversation.

Day 102

· · · · · · · · · · ·

Between the Covers

Talk about fabulous! Slipping between the
covers of a great book (preferably snuggled
in bed) is the perfect way to wind down
after a long day. There, in the comfort of
your own bedroom, you can be swept away
to worlds unknown.

Day 103

. . . .

Sharp Vision

As selfishness and complaint pervert
the mind, so love with its joy clears
and sharpens the vision.

Helen Keller

Day 104

. . . .

A Day in the Mountains

Ah, fresh air! Sunshine. Spending time
in nature, close to your Creator. Is there
anything more fabulous than a day in the
mountains to make you feel refreshed,
invigorated, and ready for a challenge?

Day 105

. . . .

Fabulously Fashionable

To be a fashionable woman is to know
yourself, know what you represent,
and know what works for you.
To be "in fashion" could be a disaster
on 90 percent of women. You are
not a page out of *Vogue*.

UNKNOWN

Day 106

Noncompetitive Relationships

Remember that feeling you used to get in junior high when you wanted to fit in? Relationships were so competitive back then. Either you were in, or you weren't. These days, a noncompetitive relationship is the only way to go. Who has time for junior-high behavior?

Day 107
. . . .
Silent Men

Women love spending time with
silent men, convinced the men are great
listeners. Whether they are or aren't,
there's still something to be said for men
who let us speak our minds without
cutting us off at the chase.

Day 108

Comfortable Shoes

Comfy house shoes. A worn pair of sneakers. Sandals that have stretched out over time. Ragged flip-flops. *Ahh!* There's nothing like a pair of comfy shoes to make you feel fabulous!

Day 109

· · · · · · · · · · ·

Feather Boa

There's something about watching a little
girl play dress-up that's so much fun.
As she slips that feather boa into place,
she lets go of inhibitions.
She is lighthearted as a feather. Maybe it's
time to slip into such a lighthearted state
of mind today. Fabulous!

Day 110

· · · · · · · · · ·

To Be or Not to Be. . .Thin?

If God had meant us to be thin,
He wouldn't have created chocolate.

UNKNOWN

Day 111
· · · · · · · · · ·
Soaking Up the Sun

Don't you love leisurely days in the sun?
Whether you're at the seashore, lounging
by the pool, or sunning in the privacy of
your own backyard, there's something
rather special about soaking up some
warmth from the sunshine. Fabulous!

Day 112

· · · · · · · · · ·

The Ex-Factor

How we deal with the "ex" factor is critical
to our survival as women. Whether it's an
ex-husband, ex-boyfriend, or ex-friend,
our attitude determines our healing.
Want your life ahead to be fabulous?
Forgive the pains from the past and let go.

Day 113

· · · · · · · · · ·

Equal Treatment

There's nothing worse than discrimination,
whether it's related to your skin color,
your gender, or your desire to worship
as you please. A really fabulous woman
expects—and gives—equal treatment to
others. Why? Because she loves them.

Day 114
· · · · · · · · · ·
Stress Relief

Each woman is unique. So are the many
ways women handle stress. Some scream.
Others crawl under the covers and take a
nap. Some get a massage. Others go for a
jog. Some pray. Others go to an aerobics
class. No matter how you choose to let it
go, getting rid of it. . .truly fabulous!

Day 115

. . . .

Carefully Chosen Clothing Items

Never wear anything that panics the cat.

P. J. O'Rourke

Day 116

TV Addictions

Okay, let's admit it, ladies. Some of us (ahem!) are addicted to certain television shows. Reality TV. Home improvement shows. Daytime dramas. Nighttime comedies. We've got our favorites, and no one is taking them away from us. Why? Because they're fabulous!

Day 117

· · · · · · · · · ·

Great-Fitting Clothes

Don't you love it when you find clothes
that fit. . .truly fit? No baggy waistlines.
No bunching in the middle. Just the right
length. Just the right width. Just the
right everything! Ah, fabulous!

Day 118

· · · · · · · · · ·

Prayer

By far the most fabulous thing we have as women is the opportunity—and blessing— to pray. When we're facing challenges or want to lift up a friend in need, prayer is the very best way to make a difference.

Day 119
· · · · · · · · · ·
Provision

There's something so fabulous about
having "just enough and just in time," isn't
there? Knowing that your "daily bread" is
covered, that the pantry has food and the
car has gas, is a terrific feeling.

Day 120

. . . .

Ah, Chocolate!

I am not overweight.
I am chocolate-enriched.

UNKNOWN

Day 121

. . . .

Photo Albums

Women love looking at photos of days
gone by. Pictures from our childhood.
Pictures of our parents at a younger age.
Pictures of friends who've moved away.
Pictures of our children or grandchildren.
Where would we be without those fabulous
photos to stir our memories?

Day 122

. . . .

Pets as Accessories

Are you one of those pet owners who loves
to dress up your dog in a cute little outfit?
These days, we can outfit our pets for
every occasion, even matching their
clothes to ours. How fun, to slip Fifi
into a cute little getup for an outing!
Dogs might be man's best friend,
but they're woman's best accessory.

Day 123

. . . .

Queen for a Day

Back in the fifties there was a television show called *Queen for a Day*. These days, you don't have to go on TV to be a queen. Women today have hair salons, spas, and a host of other places, all designed to make them feel like royalty. Fabulous!

Day 124

· · · · · · · · · ·

Turn It Around!

Stressed spelled backwards is desserts.
Coincidence? I think not!

UNKNOWN

Day 125

· · · · · · · · · · ·

Brunch

It isn't breakfast. It isn't lunch. It's that
fabulous meal in-between, where you
gather with friends, nibble on all sorts of
goodies, and talk about girl stuff.
Ah, brunch! Truly fabulous!

Day 126

· · · · · · · · · · ·

Fabulous Forgiveness

If you've ever wronged a friend and then
experienced her forgiveness, you know
the powerful release that comes on the
tail end of being forgiven. Want to know
something even more fabulous?
Extending forgiveness to others—
especially when they don't deserve it—
now that is truly fabulous.

Day 127

. . . .

A Great Pillow

If you've ever spent the night in a hotel
or at a friend's house, then you know how
miserable a bad pillow can be.
There's nothing like your own familiar
pillow. Investing in fabulous pillows might
be costly, but in the long run they can save
you money—at the chiropractor,
doctor, and more.

Day 128

. . . .

Retreating with Friends

Sometimes we need to step away from
life. Head off to a different locale.
Lay down our work for a few days.
One of the most fabulous ways to do
this is to retreat with your sister-friends.
Why not contact a retreat center and set
up a weekend getaway?

Day 129

. . . .

Income Tax Refund

The happiest day of the year?
The day the IRS deposits that refund check
into your account. It's like Christmas and
your birthday all rolled into one fabulous day.

Day 130

· · · · · · · · · ·

The Good Old Days

Life was so much easier when your clothes
didn't match and boys had cooties!

UNKNOWN

Day 131
· · · · · · · · · ·
Knowing When to Show Your Cards

A woman, especially if she has the
misfortune of knowing anything,
should conceal it as well as she can.

JANE AUSTEN

Day 132

. . . .

A Bubbly Personality

Don't you love those friends and
coworkers with bubbly personalities?
Sure, they may seem a little giddy—
or even silly—at times, but in the long
run, they keep your spirits up and
always see the glass as half full.
What a fabulous blessing they are!

Day 133

. . . .

Great Taste in Men

A truly discerning woman has great
taste—in clothes, shoes, handbags, friends,
and more. Most important, she has great
taste in men. She knows how to pick the
perfect guy, one who complements her and
brings balance to her life.

Day 134

· · · · · · · · · · ·

Beauty or Brains?

What a conundrum for the average
woman. We long for beauty, because we
have a desire to be attractive to others.
We lean on our brains, because we
know that beauty fades. Instead of
focusing on your own beauty or
intelligence today, compliment another
fabulous woman, instead.

Day 135
. . . .
What Women Want

After about twenty years of marriage,
I'm finally starting to scratch the surface
of what women want. And I think
the answer lies somewhere between
conversation and chocolate.

MEL GIBSON

Day 136

. . . .

Finding Value in People, Not Things

All around us, people put value in their
"stuff"—houses, cars, clothes, handbags,
shoes, and so on. Today, make a special
point to look for the value in the
fabulous people around you.

Day 137

. . . .

P. I. N. K.

Most girls love the color pink.
How fabulous, then, that pink has become
the designated color for breast cancer
awareness. The next time you wear pink,
may it remind you to donate. . .and to pray
for those battling for their lives.

Day 138
· · · · · · · · · · ·
The Love of a Great Guy

Oh, how wonderful to be loved by a great
guy—one who cares about your needs,
makes sure you receive his love in a way
that makes sense to your personality,
and doesn't try to squash your individuality
or uniqueness. A guy like that? Fabulous!

Day 139

. . . .

Cupcakes

Yum. . .cupcakes! Those delectable,
sweet, satisfying bits of goodness!
They're the perfect alternative to cake or
cookies and can be made in a variety of
fabulous flavors, sure to delight
friends and family.

Day 140
. . . .
Which Would You Rather Be?

I'd much rather be a woman
than a man. Women can cry,
they can wear cute clothes,
and they are the first to be
rescued off of sinking ships.

GILDA RADNER

Day 141
· · · · · · · · · ·
Those Fabulous Curves

Many of us complain because we're too curvy. We wish for a slimmer, straighter physique. Remember, curves are always in style. So, celebrate yours today!

Day 142

. . . .

A Pleasant Disposition

Is there anything lovelier than a pleasant
disposition? Even the plainest of women
resonates beauty when her disposition
is gracious and kind. Today, do a
"disposition check." Make sure your
attitude lifts others up.

Day 143

. . . .

A Fabulous Work of Fiction

A man's face is his autobiography.
A woman's face is her work of fiction.

OSCAR WILDE

Day 144

. . . .

Learning from Past Mistakes

If you're like most women, you've made
a few mistakes in your life. Okay, maybe
more than a few. How wonderful to learn
the appropriate lessons from your mistakes
and move on, stronger than before and
confident you won't make that
mistake again!

Day 145

. . . .

It's All Relative

Friends are relatives you make for yourself.

EUSTACHE DESCHAMPS

Day 146
. . . .
Singing Your Own Song

Part of what makes women so fabulous is
their ability to maintain their uniqueness,
even in a crowd. Don't try to fit in.
March to your own drumbeat.
Dance to your own rhythm. Sing your
own song. You were created to be
fabulously different, so sing your life-song
at the top of your lungs!

Day 147

. . . .

Setting Goals

Are you a goal-setter? Do you plan out
your day or make lists? It's important to
set goals, even small ones. Your chances of
hitting the target are much better if you
actually aim for it! Goals are a fabulous
way to keep your career, your life, and your
family moving toward a happy destination.

Day 148

· · · · · · · · · ·

Free Babysitters

All mothers will attest to the fact that
caring for children can be a challenge.
That's why it's great to have time away.
And there's nothing better than a free
babysitter, is there? Whether it's
Grandma, a friend from church,
 a neighbor, or a good friend,
having someone you trust
is such a blessing!

Day 149

. . . .

Love It! Hate It!

Women usually love what they buy,
yet hate two-thirds of what is
in their closets.

MIGNON MCLAUGHLIN

Day 150
. . . .
Leadership Opportunities

Life sometimes gives women the
opportunity to step up to the plate and
lead. In the business world. In politics.
In the home. In schools. Women make
strong leaders, in part because they care so
deeply about those they are leading.
How fabulous, to be a woman
who leads with love.

Day 151
. . . .
Seize the Moment

Seize the moment. Remember all
those women on the *Titanic* who
waved off the dessert cart.

Erma Bombeck

Day 152

· · · · · · · · · · ·

Killing Off the Heartbreaker

Let's face it, girls. Some of us—
especially the pretty ones—thrive on
breaking hearts. Today, make up your
mind to be a heart-mender,
not a heartbreaker.

Day 153

· · · · · · · · · ·

A Great Shampoo

Ah, shampoo! Having one you love can
make all the difference. And going to a
salon to have your hair washed by
someone else? Even better!

Day 154
. . . .
Peace of Mind

If you had all of the money in the world,
you still couldn't buy the one thing that
matters most—peace of mind. True peace
of mind only comes from one place. . .
above. And the best news of all?
It's absolutely free.

Day 155

· · · · · · · · · · · ·

Finding Your Prince

There are so many girls,
and so few princes.

LIZA MINNELLI

Day 156

. . . .

A Man Who Knows How to Grill

There's nothing more fabulous
than being a woman who gets to watch
her man cook, especially if he's grilling.
And, really, is there anything more
attractive than a man who
knows how to grill?

Day 157

. . . .

The New Gold Standard

Please allow me to offer a simple
financial plan. Invest in chocolate.
Buy bars. Lots of bars. If we do enter
anything approximating a real financial
depression, you will not be able to
improve your mood with gold.

ANITA RENFROE

Day 158

· · · · · · · · · · ·

Vulnerability

Looking for the best beauty product
around? Try vulnerability. There's nothing
more beautiful than a woman who
occasionally lets her hair down and exposes
her flaws to a watching world.

Day 159

· · · · · · · · · ·

A Woman of Character

If you've ever met a woman of character—
someone who's the real deal—you've truly
met a fabulous woman. She does what she
says she's going to do and doesn't hurt
others in the process. She won't lie, cheat,
or steal to get the job done either. Nope.
She just does it the good old-fashioned
way—with hard work.

Day 160

. . . .

Getting Fit

Don't you love the idea of being in shape?
Is there anything better? Maybe you think
it's impossible because you've already
let things go. It's never to late to start.
So. . .get fit!

Day 161

. . . .

BFF

Having a BFF is such a blessing.
These special friends stick with you
through thick and thin. They're the first
to answer your cry for help and the last to
leave when the party's over. (They stick
around to help you clean up!)
Oh, those fabulous BFFs!

Day 162
· · · · · · · · · · ·
Hiring a Maid

Oh, the joy of being able to afford a maid!
Someone to mop the floors, polish the
cabinets, and dust the furniture. Is there
anything more fabulous than passing off
those tasks to someone else?
(Even just once?) What luxury!

Day 163

· · · · · · · · · · ·

Weaker. . .or Wiser?

I have an idea that the phrase "weaker sex" was coined by some woman to disarm some man she was preparing to overwhelm.

OGDEN NASH

Day 164

A New Outfit That Makes You Look Thin

Getting a new outfit is fantastic, but getting one that makes you look thin. . .priceless! Nothing can top that "I really feel good in this outfit!" feeling. Enjoy every minute!

Day 165

. . . .

Reality Check!

Every time I close the door on reality,
it comes in through the windows.

JENNIFER UNLIMITED

Day 166
· · · · · · · · · · ·
Volunteering at a Nursing Home

Want to feel great about life?
Want to make a difference?
Try volunteering at a local nursing home.
The fabulous people you meet (workers
and senior citizens alike) will bring a smile
to your face, put a song in your heart,
and add a skip to your step.

Day 167

· · · · · · · · · ·

Great Skin

The finest clothing made is a person's skin,
but, of course, society demands
something more than this.

MARK TWAIN

Day 168

. . . .

A New House

If you've ever had the opportunity to move into a new home, you know how fabulous it can be. There's something so fresh, so invigorating, about having a blank slate. It's clean, everything's in working condition, and you can truly make it your own!

Day 169

. . . .

Lazy Saturday Mornings

Ah, the luxury! Sleeping in. Lounging
around in your pj's. Eating breakfast in
bed. Watching cartoons with the kids.
Taking your time with housework.
Those fabulous Saturday mornings are
meant to be treasured!

Day 170

Fabulous Beginnings

In the beginning, the Lord created
chocolate, and He saw that it was good.
Then He separated the light from the dark,
and it was better.

UNKNOWN

Day 171

· · · · · · · · · ·

Strong Faith

There's something so fabulous about
people with strong faith. They go through
the same trials and tribulations we go
through but seem to weather the storms
much better. What about you?
Maybe it's time to put your faith in
something—*Someone*—big enough
to handle those storms!

Day 172

. . . .

Joy in the Morning

Ever had a really rough night?
Maybe you stayed up until the wee
hours, crying your eyes out over
something that really hurt you.
There's good news! With the sunrise
comes a brand-new fabulous day!
Brush away those tears.
Morning is coming!

Day 173

The Perfect Fit

Woman was taken out of man; not out of his head to top him, nor out of his feet to be trampled underfoot; but out of his side to be equal to him, under his arm to be protected, and near his heart to be loved.

UNKNOWN

Day 174

· · · · · · · · · · ·

Saturday Afternoon with a Good Friend

Ah, Saturday! A day of rest after a long
week. And who better to spend a
luxurious Saturday with than a good
friend? Kicking back. Eating lunch.
Shopping. Going to a movie.
What a fabulous way to spend the day!

Day 175

. . . .

Time for a Tune-Up!

A male gynecologist is like an auto
mechanic who never owned a car.

CARRIE SNOW

Day 176
· · · · · · · · · · ·
The Freedom to Be Yourself

Don't you love it when you're hanging
out with people who encourage you to be
yourself? No pretense. No sucking in your
stomach. No acting a part. Just you. . .
right down to the core. What fabulous
freedom, to relax and just. . .be!

Day 177

. . . .

Happy and Fat

Can you imagine a world without men?
No crime and lots of happy fat women.

NICOLE HOLLANDER

Day 178
. . . .
Friends with Thick Skin

Oy! Don't you go a little crazy when your
friends overreact to things? Sometimes
their skin is way too thin! That's why it's
such a blessing to hang out with a
thick-skinned friend. She can take critique
and not knee-jerk. She doesn't get her
feelings wounded at every little thing and
laughs off the potentially hurtful stuff.

Day 179

. . . .

Friends with a Sense of Humor

What a blast, to share a few hours with a
great friend who has a fabulous sense of
humor. You can share stories with laughter
ringing out every step of the way. A good
friend is a treasure. A good friend with a
sense of humor? Priceless!

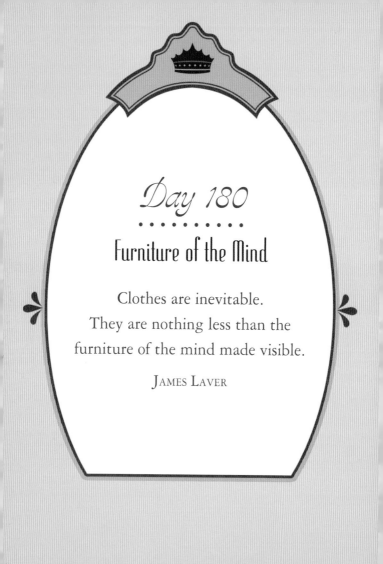

Day 180

· · · · · · · · · ·

Furniture of the Mind

Clothes are inevitable.
They are nothing less than the
furniture of the mind made visible.

JAMES LAVER

Day 181
. . . .
Creativity

Creativity is truly a fabulous gift from
above. It stirs us to do things we didn't
think we could do and to express ourselves
in ways we never thought we could.

Day 182

· · · · · · · · · ·

ROFL

Have you ever had such a great time
with a girlfriend that you felt like ROFL
(rolling on the floor laughing)?
Remember when you were a teen and you
would get so tickled that you couldn't stop
laughing, no matter how hard you tried?
It's not too late to ROFL right now,
even as an adult. What a fabulous way
to ease the tensions of life!

Day 183
· · · · · · · · · · ·
Advice from Mama

When your mother asks, "Do you want
a piece of advice?" it is a mere formality.
It doesn't matter if you answer yes or no.
You're going to get it anyway.

Erma Bombeck

Day 184

· · · · · · · · · ·

Beautiful Artwork

Talk about inspiring! Fabulous
artwork does more than dress up a room
or hallway. It inspires us to dream, to hope,
to create. When we choose the artwork
to fill our space, we have the
opportunity to show
a sliver of our personality.

Day 185
. . . .
You Don't Need to Say It

Silences make the real conversations
between friends. Not the saying, but the
never needing to say is what counts.

MARGARET LEE RUNBECK

Day 186
. . . .
Covering Up the Gray

Whether you choose to cover up your gray
hair or not, you can still choose to cover
the "gray" areas of your life. Those "blah"
moments can really get you down, so cover
them—with grace, with a smile,
and with a great sense of humor.

Day 187

· · · · · · · · · · ·

A Fix-It Guy

There's nothing better than a great guy,
except perhaps a guy with a tool belt
strapped on. There's something pretty
fabulous about a man who knows how to
play the role of fix-it guy when necessary.

Day 188

Say Good-Bye to Manipulation

Love comes when manipulation stops; when you think more about the other person than about his or her reactions to you. When you dare to reveal yourself fully. When you dare to be vulnerable.

DR. JOYCE BROTHERS

Day 189
. . . .
Choose Your Own Style

Instead of following trends or dressing
like everyone else in your circle of friends,
spend some time analyzing the colors
and styles that work for you. Having the
courage to choose your own style
is truly fabulous.

Day 190

. . . .

Childhood Memories

Don't you love those fabulous childhood
memories? The "good old days" were likely
filled with fun adventures with friends,
popsicles, puppy dogs, kitty cats,
bobby socks, and icky boys with cooties.
Okay, your opinion of boys has changed,
but those other memories are priceless!

Day 191

· · · · · · · · · ·

An Ageless Mind-Set

Age is not measured by years.
Nature does not equally distribute energy.
Some people are born old and tired while
others are going strong at seventy.

DOROTHY THOMPSON

Day 192

· · · · · · · · · · ·

A Day in the Tropics

When you dream of going to the tropics,
what locale comes to mind? Hawaii?
St. Thomas? Cancun? Cozumel?
The Bahamas? Even if you can't travel
to one of these fabulous, exotic locations,
you can enjoy a day in the sun with your
family. Use a coconut-scented tanning oil.
It will make you feel like
you're headed to the beach!

Day 193

. . . .

Rekindling the Inner Spirit

In everyone's life, at some time, our inner
fire goes out. It is then burst into flame
by an encounter with another human
being. We should all be thankful for those
people who rekindle the inner spirit.

ALBERT SCHWEITZER

Day 194

. . . .

Glimpses of Heaven

Don't you enjoy the little glimpses of
heaven we get here on earth? A child's
smile. A sweet conversation with a senior
citizen. A heavenly scent. An afternoon
surrounded by nature at its finest.
Truly, those little glimpses give us hope
that the real thing will far surpass
what we already see.

Day 195

. . . .

Sugar Substitutes

Let's face it. . .most of us are sugar addicts. We put it in our coffee, our tea, our desserts, our snacks. It's even in our salad dressing. Perhaps you're counting calories. If so, then you're probably very grateful for sugar substitutes. They offer the same sweetness without the calories or carbs. Fabulous!

Day 196

. . . .

I Believe. . .

I believe in manicures.
I believe in overdressing.
I believe in primping at leisure and
wearing lipstick. I believe in pink.
I believe happy girls are the
prettiest girls.
I believe that tomorrow
is another day, and. . .
I believe in miracles.

AUDREY HEPBURN

Day 197

· · · · · · · · · · ·

A Great Cell Phone

These days, cell phones aren't just
necessities, they're accessories.
Adorned with pink cases, fabulous apps,
and cool ringtones, they are truly
a reflection of our sense of style and
unique personality.

Day 198

· · · · · · · · · ·

Great Ethnic Cuisine

Whether it's Chinese, Mexican, Italian, Vietnamese, Japanese, Indian, or Tex-Mex, twenty-first-century women just can't get enough of that fabulous ethnic food! In a sense, you're traveling the world when you experience a meal from a different culture. And it's so tasty, too!

Day 199

· · · · · · · · · ·

Butterfly Kisses

Whether they're from a grandchild, a son
or daughter, a niece or nephew, or a child
in the nursery where you volunteer,
there's nothing like a butterfly kiss from a
child. Those sweet eyelash kisses will sweep
you away to a simpler time and place and
remind you of the innocence
and wonder of childhood.

Day 200

· · · · · · · · · · ·

An Enchanting Creature

Just around the corner in every woman's
mind is a lovely dress, a wonderful suit,
or entire costume which will make an
enchanting new creature of her.

WILHELA CUSHMAN

Day 201

. . . .

Tip toeing through the Tulips

Some women have the ability to tread lightly through situations, careful to protect things of value and other people. It's a fabulous feat, to have a gentle spirit, especially when others around you plow through situations like bulls in a china shop.

Day 202

Healthy Eating

Healthy eating is more than just a fad
or something fun to do to get attention.
It's critical to our health and the health of
our family. Want to look and feel fabulous?
Fuel your body with fabulous,
healthy food.

Day 203

· · · · · · · · · · · ·

A Love of Books

There are many little ways to
enlarge your child's world.
Love of books is the best of all.

JACQUELINE KENNEDY ONASSIS

Day 204

· · · · · · · · · ·

Good Directions

Whether you're sitting in the
driver's seat or on the passenger side,
there's nothing like great directions.
Knowing where you're going—and how
to get there—is critical. And while we
wouldn't come out and say that the
men in our lives are directionless,
we could say it's a mighty good
thing we're along for the ride.

Day 205

· · · · · · · · · · ·

Your Most Powerful Charm

When a girl ceases to blush, she has lost
the most powerful charm of her beauty.

POPE GREGORY I

Day 206
· · · · · · · · · · ·
Open Doors

We're always looking for direction in
our lives, which is why it's so fabulous
when doors swing wide open. They usher
us into new places, new possibilities,
new adventures. Oh, how we love
those open doors!

Day 207

Caring for Those in the Military

One of the most fabulous things we can do is to care about (and pray for) those in our military. They give up so much to serve us. Giving back is the least we can do!

Day 208

. . . .

Hats

In generations gone by, hats were crucial
parts of a woman's wardrobe. These days,
they're considered an occasional accessory.
But, oh. . .what fun! Hats transform us in
a hurry. We can go from being a diva to
a cowgirl to a sports enthusiast,
just by changing our hat!

Day 209
. . . .
Give Yourself a Break!

That's when the great stuff happens,
when you're not checking yourself all the
time, being critical of yourself and what
other people are doing.

CAROL KANE

Day 210
· · · · · · · · · ·
No Payment, Please

You can't live a perfect day without
doing something for someone who
will never be able to repay you.

JOHN WOODEN

Day 211
. . . .
A Child's Smile

Chubby dimpled cheeks.
Perfect little teeth. A silly crooked grin.
Giggling laughter, rippling across the
room. Really, is there anything more
delightful than a child's smile?

Day 212

· · · · · · · · · ·

Thoughts on Fame

Fame will go by and, so long, I've had
you, fame. If it goes by, I've always
known it was fickle. So at least it's
something I experience,
but that's not where I live.

MARILYN MONROE

Day 213

· · · · · · · · · ·

The Perfect Pair of Heels

Our closets are filled with shoes,
both practical and impractical.
Of all the shoes we own, there's that one
really snazzy pair of heels, the ones we
pull out when we mean business. When
we have worlds to conquer, we do it in our
best heels. Why? Because they're fabulous!

Day 214

· · · · · · · · · ·

Seeing the Glass as Half Full

Are you a glass-half-full sort of girl?
Does your positive spirit always look for
the best, the most hopeful, the positive
in situations and people? If so, then your
contagious attitude spills out on others.
They glean from your positivity and see
you as an encouragement in their lives.

Day 215

· · · · · · · · · ·

Chocoholics Alert!

The Twelve-Step Chocoholics
Program: Never be more than twelve
steps away from chocolate!

TERRY MOORE

Day 216

. . . .

Paid Bills

If you've ever walked through a "barely
scraping by" season, then you can
appreciate the blessing of knowing the bills
are paid. It's a fabulous feeling,
not to owe anyone. Electric bill? Paid!
Car payment? Paid! Mortgage? Paid!
Credit cards? Paid! There. . .
see how good that feels?

Day 217

. . . .

Extending a Hand

As you grow older, you will discover
that you have two hands, one for helping
yourself, the other for helping others.

AUDREY HEPBURN

Day 218
· · · · · · · · · ·
Reconnecting with an Old Friend

Don't you love social media sites?
They're great for staying in touch with
the people in your world, but they're also
a great way to track down friends you
haven't seen in years. There's truly nothing
more fabulous than reconnecting with a
girlfriend from the past.

Day 219

· · · · · · · · · ·

Senseless Chatter

Sometimes a girl's just gotta do what
a girl's gotta do, even if it seems a little
senseless to others. Chatting with friends—
even pointless, silly chatting—is often just
the thing we need to take
our mind off of things.

Day 220

· · · · · · · · · · ·

Our Best Twenty!

When we lose twenty pounds. . .
we may be losing the twenty best
pounds we have! We may be losing the
pounds that contain our genius,
our humanity, our love and honesty.

WOODY ALLEN

Day 221

. . . .

Opportunity Knocks!

Do you ever get that sense of anticipation,
the one that says, "Something big is
coming!" And then. . .*bam!* You're faced
with an opportunity, one that changes
your life forever. How fabulous,
those unexpected blessings!

Day 222

Allowing Yourself to Be Loved

I think that the most difficult thing is
allowing yourself to be loved, so receiving
the love and feeling like you deserve it is
a pretty big struggle. I suppose that's
what I've learned recently, to allow
myself to be loved.

NICOLE KIDMAN

Day 223

Finding a Great Bargain

Don't you love finding a great bargain?
There's something pretty fabulous about
getting something at a really great price.
Good bargains are hard to come by,
especially in today's economy, but a savvy
shopper knows just where to find them.
She's on the prowl, always looking
for the best deal.

Day 224
. . . .

An Optimistic Sunrise

After five thousand years of recorded
human history, you wonder, what part
of two million sunrises doesn't a
pessimist understand?

ROBERT BRAULT

Day 225
. . . .
A Great Parking Spot

Imagine this: You're in a rush. Just arrived
at the store. The parking lot is full.
Not one space available. You're about to give
up when a car pulls out of the perfect spot,
leaving it open for you. Fabulous timing!

Day 226

. . . .

Blowing Kisses

Friends are kisses blown to us by angels.

UNKNOWN

Day 227

. . . .

Eating Breakfast for Dinner

Want to have a truly fabulous evening
meal? Try pancakes. Or, better yet,
waffles and bacon. Maybe an omelet.
There's something so fun about having
breakfast at night. It breaks the rules
(Who made those rules, anyway?)
and it's yummy and satisfying.

Day 228

· · · · · · · · · ·

Courage

Courage is the most important of all
the virtues, because without courage
you can't practice any other virtue
consistently. You can practice any
virtue erratically, but nothing
consistently without courage.

MAYA ANGELOU

Day 229

. . . .

Parties

Don't you love throwing parties?
Some women will use any excuse to host
one! Whether it's a birthday,
bridal shower, holiday, or fun girlfriend
get-together, putting together a great
party can be a fabulous way to use
your creative skills.

Day 230

· · · · · · · · · ·

Inspirational Movies

Grab the tissues and prepare yourself for
the inevitable. An inspirational movie—
one that encourages, uplifts, and touches
the heart—often leads us to tears, as well.
When you find a really fabulous movie
that inspires you, you'll watch it again. . .
and again. . .and again!

Day 231
· · · · · · · · · · ·
Thankfulness

Be thankful for what you have; you'll end
up having more. If you concentrate on
what you don't have, you will never,
ever have enough.

OPRAH WINFREY

Day 232

· · · · · · · · · · ·

Rocky Road Ice Cream

Smooth. Creamy. Crunchy. Sweet.
All words to describe that fabulous treat—
Rocky Road ice cream. It's the perfect
antidote to life's woes.

Day 233
· · · · · · · · · · ·
Speaking Through the Silence

A girlfriend is probably the only person
in this world who understands exactly
what you are saying even though you
may not really be talking.

UNKNOWN

Day 234

· · · · · · · · · · ·

A Good Woman

If I were a girl, I'd despair.
The supply of good women far exceeds
that of the men who deserve them.

ROBERT GRAVES

Day 235

. . . .

A Good Foundation

Oh, how we love to cover up our flaws.
We reach for a good foundation to
smooth out discolored skin and cover
imperfections. While you're at it,
make sure your life has a strong
foundation. What's the point of
a near-perfect face with a life
on shaky ground?

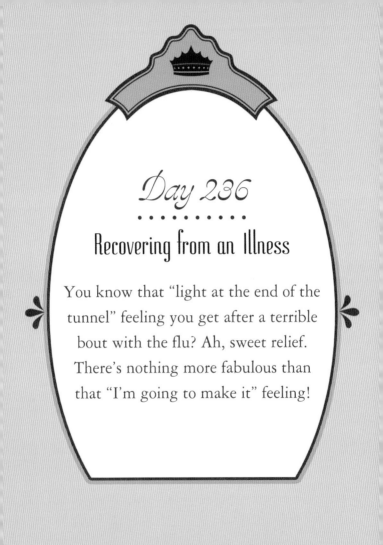

Day 236

Recovering from an Illness

You know that "light at the end of the tunnel" feeling you get after a terrible bout with the flu? Ah, sweet relief. There's nothing more fabulous than that "I'm going to make it" feeling!

Day 237

· · · · · · · · · · ·

Falling In!

Forget love,
I'd rather fall in chocolate!

SANDRA J. DYKES

Day 238

. . . .

A Drop in Gas Prices

When gas prices are high, tempers can
get even higher! There's something pretty
fabulous about driving by the gas station
and noticing that prices have dropped.

Day 239

· · · · · · · · · · ·

Going on a Cruise

Oh, what fun! Cruising from location to location with a friend or loved one can be the ideal vacation. Where else can you see so many different ports of call and eat such delicious food? What a fabulous way to spend your holiday!

Day 240
· · · · · · · · · · ·
A True Gentleman

Is there anything more inspiring than a
true gentleman? He opens the car door for
you, pulls out your chair, offers genuine,
heartfelt flattery at just the right moment.
His manner is calm, cool, and collected,
and his smile will win your heart every
time. If and when you find
such a man, snatch him up!

Day 241
. . . .
People Who Sparkle and Shine

People are like stained-glass windows.
They sparkle and shine when the sun is
out, but when the darkness sets in their
true beauty is revealed only if
there is light from within.

ELISABETH KÜBLER-ROSS

Day 242
. . . .
A Good Doctor

Finding a doctor you trust—one who gives
you accurate diagnoses and workable plans
to overcome obstacles—is so important to
women. A truly fabulous doctor will make
room for you in his or her busy schedule
and give you the tools you need to be
in the best possible health.

Day 243

· · · · · · · · · ·

Barbie Dilemma

If Barbie is so popular,
why do people have to buy her friends?

UNKNOWN

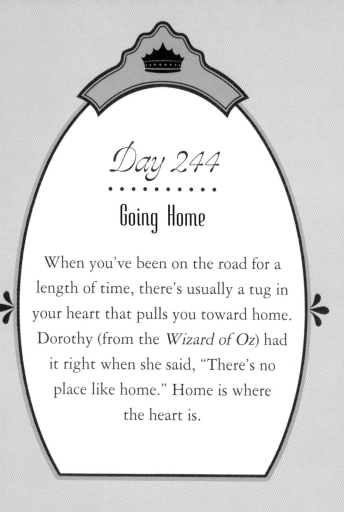

Day 244

· · · · · · · · · · ·

Going Home

When you've been on the road for a
length of time, there's usually a tug in
your heart that pulls you toward home.
Dorothy (from the *Wizard of Oz*) had
it right when she said, "There's no
place like home." Home is where
the heart is.

Day 245

. . . .

Lend Me Your Ear

There is no greater loan
than a sympathetic ear.

FRANK TYGER

Day 246

· · · · · · · · · · ·

Walks along the Beach

What woman doesn't like to walk along
the beach, bare feet leaving imprints in the
sand? There's just something about the
majesty of the water, the squishy feeling
of sand between the toes, and the smell
of salt in the air that's truly fabulous!

Day 247

· · · · · · · · · · ·

Eleventh-Hour Miracles

If you've ever been through a really
difficult time in your life—a time when it
seemed like things weren't going to work
out—then you can appreciate the joy of an
eleventh-hour miracle. These "seemingly
impossible" miracles usually come just in
time. Crisis averted! Miraculous!

Day 248

· · · · · · · · · · ·

Connection to Life

A good friend is a connection to life—
a tie to the past, a road to the future,
the key to sanity in a totally insane world.

LOIS WYSE

Day 249
. . . .
The Rainbow after a Storm

If you've ever looked up in the sky after
a rainstorm to discover a brilliant rainbow,
then you know the feeling of hope that
envelops you. You really can go on after
life's storms, even when it feels impossible.
The rainbow is a sign, a colorful bow
of hope, urging you to put one foot
in front of the other.

Day 250
. . . .
Doing the Impossible

When someone says, "It can't be done,"
how do you respond? Do you tuck your
tail between your legs and walk away,
defeated? Of course not! A truly fabulous
woman finds a way to get things done,
even when it seems impossible.

Day 251
. . . .
A Reflection of the Heart

Adornment is never anything
except a reflection of the heart.

Coco Chanel

Day 252

. . . .

A Sense of Anticipation

There's something so wonderful
about having a sense of anticipation.
You're counting down the days,
convinced fabulous things are ahead.
Sometimes it's hard to know which is
more fun—arriving at your
destination, or the sense of
expectation along the way!

Day 253
· · · · · · · · · ·
Our Secret Source of Power

Guys, a woman's purse, alright,
it's her secret source of power. . . .
There are many dark and dangerous things
in there that we, the male species,
should know nothing about.

BEN, *HOW TO LOSE A GUY IN TEN DAYS*

Day 254

. . . .

An Infectious Smile

Don't you love a person with an infectious smile? Maybe you're having a terrible day and you pass by an elderly person in the grocery store. She flashes you a bright smile. Or maybe you're fit to be tied with your toddler and he grins at you with that little toothy grin of his. You melt like butter. Yep, there's something pretty magical about a smile!

Day 255

· · · · · · · · · ·

Good Architecture

Fashion is architecture:
it is a matter of proportions.

COCO CHANEL

Day 256

. . . .

Joy-Choosers

If you're like most women, you have a
wide variety of friends. Some are positive
and upbeat. Others are, frankly,
real downers. Truly, the best kind of
friend is the one who chooses joy, even in
the midst of pain. She's real about the pain
but doesn't wallow in it. Are you that
kind of friend to others?

Day 257

. . . .

Bridal Showers

Don't you love a great bridal shower?
The sense of anticipation permeates the
room as the bride-to-be giggles her way
through the event. Her thoughts?
They're on the big day, of course. But in
the meantime, the ladies can laugh their
way past the lingerie, the gift registry
items, and the chatter about
the honeymoon night.

Day 258

· · · · · · · · · ·

Purr-fectly Great!

If I were a cat, what would make me purr? A pair of really comfortable blue jeans and massages.

CINNAMON STOMBERGER

Day 259
· · · · · · · · · ·
Wishing and Hoping

Remember when you were a little girl
and you would wish upon a star?
What was your greatest desire?
For your wish to come true, of course!
There's something pretty fabulous about
wishing and hoping. It leads to a sense
of anticipation and excitement about
the future. So, wish away!

Day 260

· · · · · · · · · · ·

Models

The leading cause of death among fashion models is falling through street grates.

DAVE BARRY

Day 261

· · · · · · · · · ·

Giggling

Have you ever walked by a room filled
with little girls and heard them giggling
together? That sound is magical, isn't it?
It's contagious. Giggling is a gift. It rises
from the inside and bubbles out for all to
hear. Don't hold those giggles inside.
Set them free!

Day 262

· · · · · · · · · ·

Following Your Aspirations

Far away there in the sunshine are my
highest aspirations. I may not reach them,
but I can look up and see their beauty,
believe in them, and try to follow
where they lead.

LOUISA MAY ALCOTT

Day 263

. . . .

Sitting on the Porch Swing
with Someone You Love

Ah, pure delight! Sitting on the porch
swing in the early evening. Watching
the sun set with someone you love at your
side. Listening to the sounds of nature as
day slips into night. Is there anything
more fabulous?

Day 264

. . . .

To Weigh. . .or Not to Weigh?

In the Middle Ages, they had
guillotines, stretch racks, whips,
and chains. Nowadays, we have a much
more effective torture device called
the bathroom scale.

STEPHEN PHILLIPS

Day 265

· · · · · · · · · · ·

Sharing Dessert (and Calories) with a Friend

When we were kids, we didn't like to share. However, as adults, we've learned that sharing—especially sweet desserts loaded with calories—is the perfect solution! We really can have our cake and eat it, too. . .as long as we share it with a friend!

Day 266

. . . .

Putting the Kids Down for a Nap

It's been a long morning. You're at
your wit's end. The kids have eaten
lunch and you're ready for that magic
moment when you put them down for
a nap. Minutes later they're snoozing and
you're chillin', putting your feet up,
and thanking God for a few minutes
of rest. Gotta love those naps!

Day 267

. . . .

Social Media Birthdays

Remember what birthdays were like
before you had a social media site?
You wondered if anyone even remembered
you. Now you get tweets, Facebook posts,
Myspace acknowledgments, and even blog
comments. Happy birthday to you—
a thousand times over!

Day 268

· · · · · · · · · ·

Arms to Wrap around Others

A hug delights and warms and charms—
that must be why God gave us arms.

UNKNOWN

Day 269

. . . .

Ocean Waves

There's nothing more majestic than the
ocean, especially at high tide.
Standing at the water's edge, you can
almost feel the push and pull of the waves.
They're a reminder that Someone much
greater has all of this in the palm of
His hand. Knowing we can trust Him?
Fabulous!

Day 270

· · · · · · · · · · ·

Let's Binge!

Life itself is the proper binge.

JULIA CHILD

Day 271
The Birth of a Baby

Everyone celebrates the birth of a baby.
There's something so fabulous about
knowing two individuals have merged
to form this special little life. Staring into
that newborn's eyes, we're convinced the
circle of life really does go on
. . .and on. . .and on. . . .

Day 272

I'll Be...

If you're alone, I'll be your shadow.
If you want to cry, I'll be your shoulder.
If you want a hug, I'll be your pillow.
If you need to be happy, I'll be your smile.
But anytime you need a friend,
I'll just be me.

UNKNOWN

Day 273

Delayed Answers to Prayer

Sometimes we get bummed over what
we perceive to be unanswered prayers.
We want what we want when we want it.
Oh, how wonderful hindsight can be.
We look back, months or years later,
to discover the truth: God was protecting
us by not giving us what we asked for.

Day 274

. . . .

A Friend Who Offers Great Advice

Is there anything—or anyone—
more fabulous than a friend who comes
equipped with great advice? She knows
just what to say and when to say it.
She's not pushy. Doesn't get in your face.
Doesn't lecture. She simply speaks a few
words of truth, and they resonate within.

Day 275
. . . .
Money Talks. Chocolate Sings.

If you really want to impress a woman,
bring her chocolate. Sure, she's keen
on other nice things. But what
really makes her day is a box of
delicious chocolates. Yum!

Day 276

. . . .

Teaching a Child to Ride a Bike

Is there anything more delightful than watching a child learn to ride a bicycle for the first time? He teeters back and forth during the training wheel stage, then soars once those training wheels come off. What a great illustration of life. Like that child, we're set free to soar once we let go and trust.

Day 277

A Dewy Morning

Have you ever marveled at the glistening of early morning dew on the grass? It's as if someone turned on a heavenly sprinkler during the night, adding just the right amount of moisture to keep things going. What a lovely way to start each new day!

Day 278

· · · · · · · · · · ·

Rearranging the Furniture

There's something very invigorating about
the process of rearranging the furniture.
Moving the sofa from this wall to that
wall might not seem like a big deal,
but doing so can affect you emotionally.
It lifts you out of a rut, spiffs up the room,
and makes you see things in a whole new light.

Day 279

· · · · · · · · · ·

A Clean Car

For those with small children, a clean
car might seem like an impossibility.
Even those with teens know the struggle
of keeping things tidy. Still, there's nothing
more inviting than a clean car—top to
bottom, side to side, inside and out.
What a fabulous invitation to go for a ride!

Day 280
. . . .
Déjà Vu

I have gained and lost the same ten
pounds so many times over and over
again my cellulite must have déjà vu.

JANE WAGNER

Day 281

· · · · · · · · · · ·

Facing Your Giants

If you've ever garnered the courage to face
a huge obstacle—something you knew
could take you down in a hurry—
then you know what little David must've
felt like as he faced the mighty Goliath.
There's something pretty fabulous about
working up the courage to stand strong,
even when everything is against you.

Day 282
. . . .
Hot Chocolate

There's something pretty fabulous
about a mug filled with hot cocoa on
a cold winter's day. Add a couple of
marshmallows to the top and settle back
in your easy chair for a cozy getaway
from life's troubles. Yum!
Doesn't that taste good?

Day 283

· · · · · · · · · · ·

Mammogram Day: Breast Friends Day

One of the most fabulous things about
being female is our camaraderie.
That spirit of togetherness extends to
even the most unusual things. . .
like getting a mammogram. And why not?
We're in this together, after all!
Our new motto? Girlfriends don't let
girlfriends go without a mammogram.

Day 284

. . . .

A Good Bra

There's nothing more miserable than
a poorly fitted bra. Granted, this isn't
something we shout from the rooftops,
but maybe it should be. Finding a truly
fabulous bra—one that fits like it was
made for you—can make your day,
your week, your year.

Day 285

. . . .

Do What He Can't

A man's got to do what a man's got to do.
A woman must do what he can't.

RHONDA HANSOME

Day 286

· · · · · · · · · ·

Fashion

Art produces ugly things which
frequently become beautiful with time.
Fashion, on the other hand,
produces beautiful things which always
become ugly with time.

JEAN COCTEAU

Day 287

· · · · · · · · · · ·

Dancing to Fifties Music

Most women—even those who claim they
don't like to dance—can't keep their toes
from tapping when music from the fifties
comes on. Elvis. Jerry Lee. Dean Martin.
Pat Boone. The Platters. Doris Day.
Connie Francis. Turn up the jukebox,
ladies! It's time to hit the floor!

Day 288

· · · · · · · · · · ·

Animal Lovers

If it's true that men are such beasts,
this must account for the fact that
most women are animal lovers.

DORIS DAY

Day 289

. . . .

Making It from Scratch

Make it from scratch, you say?
Sure, why not! It takes time to make
something from scratch, but it's worth it!
It will taste better, be better for you,
and give you the satisfaction of a job well
done. What's more fabulous than that?

Day 290
· · · · · · · · · · ·
Changing Your Mind

A woman's mind is cleaner than a man's—
that's because she changes it more often.

UNKNOWN

Day 291
· · · · · · · · · · ·
Beautiful Weather

A beautiful, sunny day is such a blessing.
There's nothing better to put you in a
fabulous frame of mind than clear skies
and moderate temperatures. Flying kites.
Having a picnic with the kids. Fishing.
Ah, pure delight!

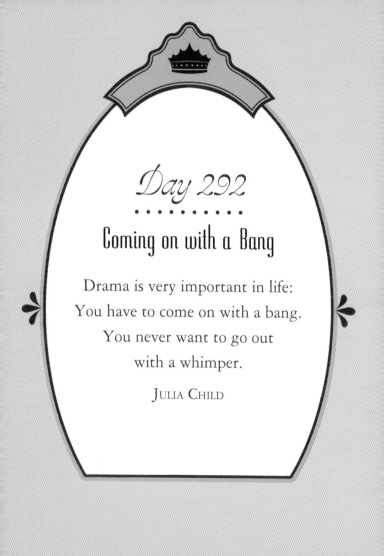

Day 292

. . . .

Coming on with a Bang

Drama is very important in life:
You have to come on with a bang.
You never want to go out
with a whimper.

JULIA CHILD

Day 293

· · · · · · · · · · · ·

A Spoonful of Sugar

A little sugar goes a long way, especially
when you add it to something bitter.
Every woman knows that the same is true
for our conversation. When things get
testy—say, someone begins to gossip—
you can turn things around in a hurry
with a few sweet words.

Day 294

. . . .

A Bouquet of Roses

Imagine you've had a rough day.
You're in a foul mood. Nothing can make
things right again. Then you receive an
unexpected delivery from the florist—
a dozen roses! Suddenly all is right with
the world again. Those flowers,
delicate and aromatic, lift your spirits and
put you in a happy place.

Day 295

· · · · · · · · · ·

A Tide That Turns

When you get into a tight place,
and everything goes against you till it
seems as if you couldn't hold on a minute
longer, never give up then, for that's just
the place and time that the tide will turn.

HARRIET BEECHER STOWE

Day 296

. . . .

A Cheerful Disposition

I am determined to be cheerful and happy
in whatever situation I may find myself.
For I have learned that the greater part
of our misery or unhappiness is
determined not by our circumstance
but by our disposition.

MARTHA WASHINGTON

Day 297
. . . .
Girls Who Wear Glasses. . .

Looking for the perfect accessory,
one sure to grab attention?
Look no further than a trendy pair
of glasses with cool colors, shapes, or bling.
There's nothing like a great pair of glasses
to draw attention to your beautiful eyes.
They're the perfect accessory!

Day 298

· · · · · · · · · · ·

An Unstoppable Attitude

The question isn't who is going to let me;
it's who is going to stop me.

AYN RAND

Day 299

. . . .

A Roaring Fire on a
Cold Winter's Night

What a wonderful, cozy feeling,
to sit in front of a roaring fire on a cold
night. Add a good book and a cup of hot
cocoa, and the evening is near to perfect!

Day 300

• • • • • • • • • •

Call Me Anytime

It is the friends you can
call up at 4 a.m. that matter.

MARLENE DIETRICH

Day 301

. . . .

Rejecting Rejection

We all face rejection. It's tough. We think
we're accepted, only to find out otherwise.
Want some fabulous advice for dealing
with rejection? Reject it! Let it go.
Don't wallow in self-pity or try to
analyze it. Just forgive those who
hurt you and move on.

Day 302

· · · · · · · · · ·

Turn On the Tears

Every woman is wrong until she cries,
and then she is right—instantly.

THOMAS CHANDLER HALIBURTON

Day 303

· · · · · · · · · · ·

A European Vacation

What do you think of when you hear
the words *European vacation*?
Sounds divine, right? Maybe you're saving
for a trip to Italy or England, Germany or
France. Perhaps Ireland is your destination
of choice. No matter where you plan to
travel, a trip to Europe sounds fabulous!

Day 304

· · · · · · · · · · ·

Romantic Notions

A romantic is one who is given
over to thoughts and feelings of love.
They're idealistic and soulful. Might seem
a little impractical, but romantics impact
our world with their art, poetry, novels,
movies, and plays. Where would we
be without romantic notions?

Day 305

· · · · · · · · · · ·

Hello, Friend!

The older you get, the tougher it is to lose
weight, because by then your body and
your fat are really good friends.

UNKNOWN

Day 306

. . . .

Powder and Paint

There's an old saying that goes like this:
"Powder and paint make a girl what she
ain't." So true! But aren't you glad we've
got the option of beautifying ourselves?
What would we do without the option
of makeup? (Many of us shiver
just thinking of it!)

Day 307

. . . .

Perfect Timing

There's nothing better than perfect timing.
Maybe you've been hoping for a new job
and an opportunity comes at the perfect
time. Maybe you thought you'd never
find Mr. Right and he waltzed into your
life at the perfect time. Waiting for the
"perfect" time can be tough,
but it's so worth it in the end!

Day 308

· · · · · · · · · · ·

Keeping a Comic Attitude

Life can be wildly tragic at times,
and I've had my share. But whatever
happens to you, you have to keep
a slightly comic attitude.
In the final analysis, you have
got not to forget to laugh.

KATHARINE HEPBURN

Day 309

. . . .

A New Hairdo

A cute, trendy style. Short. Long.
Wavy. Straight. Something different from
before. Getting a new "do" can change
your entire outlook on life. Suddenly you
feel pretty again. Younger. Hipper.
Ready to face the world. What a
fabulous mood enhancer!

Day 310

· · · · · · · · · ·

Diamonds!

Big girls need big diamonds.

ELIZABETH TAYLOR

Day 311

· · · · · · · · · ·

A "Just in Time" Note of Encouragement

Don't you love those "just in time"
notes from friends? They usually come at
the very moment you need encouragement
and say just what you need to hear.
Friends who are paying close attention hear
the cries of our heart, even when we don't
say a word. Their insight is truly fabulous.

Day 312
· · · · · · · · · ·
Freshly Painted Walls

If you've recently given one of the rooms
in your home a face-lift, then you can
appreciate the splendor of a freshly
painted wall. It's a chance to start fresh.
Begin again. Reanalyze how the room will
look for the next phase of your life.
Enjoy that new beginning!

Day 313

· · · · · · · · · ·

Self-Confidence

While clothes may not make the woman,
they certainly have a strong effect on
her self-confidence—which, I believe,
does make the woman.

MARY KAY ASHE

Day 314
. . . .
Discovering the Real Pleasures in Life

A tall glass of iced tea. A wink from the
one you love. A baby's cooing. A gorgeous
sunset. The last nibble of fudge. An email
from an old friend. These "pleasures"
aren't costly, and yet they're worth
everything in the world to us.

Day 315

. . . .

Dieting Humor

I bought a talking refrigerator that said
"Oink" every time I opened the door.
It made me hungry for pork chops.

MARIE MOTT

Day 316

Don't Worry, Be Happy

Remember that joyous little tune,
"Don't worry, be happy!" It went around
the globe, lifting spirits from country to
country. Might sound simplistic, but the
message is true: When you refuse to
worry. . .when you choose happiness. . .
the joy that follows will spread to
those around you. What a
fabulous attitude!

Day 317

· · · · · · · · · ·

Spiritual GPS

It's one thing to have a navigator in your
car or on your phone; it's a different thing
altogether to have an internal spiritual
navigator—one that points you in the
right direction at a fork in the road.
Women with spiritual depth are truly
fabulous from the inside out.

Day 318

Letting Go

Even though you may want to move forward in your life, you may have one foot on the brakes. In order to be free, we must learn how to let go. Release the hurt. Release the fear. Refuse to entertain your old pain. The energy it takes to hang onto the past is holding you back from a new life. What is it you would let go of today?

MARY MANIN MORRISSEY

Day 319
· · · · · · · · · ·
Someone Else Doing the Cooking

Let's face it. . .cooking gets old.
Whether you live alone or cook for a large
family, the task of preparing food can get
tiresome. That's why it's so fabulous to
have someone else step in and cook on
occasion. What a treat!

Day 320

Nothing Better. . .or Is There?

There is nothing better than a good friend,
except a good friend with chocolate.

UNKNOWN

Day 321

. . . .

Waking Up Early

Don't you love those fabulous days when
you wake up, roll over to look at the clock,
and realize you still have an hour to sleep?
What a wonderful feeling, to pull the
covers back over your head and doze off.
Fabulous!

Day 322

. . . .

Quiet Morning
(with a Great Cup of Coffee)

The birds are chirping outside your
window. The dew is still fresh on the grass.
You're spending those first few moments
of the day alone with a cup of coffee in
your hand, trying to wake up. In this hazy,
lazy state of mind, you're keenly aware of
the beauty—and the potential—of the day.

Day 323

. . . .

Scented Candles

Isn't it funny to think that candles—
once a necessity in every home—are now
decorative items? Candles are great on
many levels. A yummy-scented one can
change your attitude in a hurry.
The flickering light is calming. The scent
is heavenly. The mood in the room
changes immediately. Fabulous!

Day 324

. . . .

A Nail-Biter Ball Game

If you've ever watched a "down-to-the-last-minute" ball game, you know the adrenaline rush that goes along with it. What a fabulous sense of excitement fills the room as your team takes the ball in the final seconds of the game. And how awesome, when the nail-biting ends and your team rules the day!

Day 325

. . . .

Help! I Need Chocolate!

Seven days without
chocolate makes one weak.

UNKNOWN

Day 326

· · · · · · · · · · ·

A Rainy Day

Rainy days aren't as dreary as they're made
out to be. In fact, a rainy day provides a
fabulous excuse to sleep in, lounge around
in your pj's, read a book, or just enjoy the
pitter-patter of raindrops on the rooftop.

Day 327

· · · · · · · · · · ·

Shopping with a Friend

"Let's go to the mall!" Don't you love those words? They're especially wonderful coming from a good friend who knows and appreciates your shopping patterns.

Day 328

· · · · · · · · · · ·

A Nearsighted Man

Cosmetics is a boon to every woman, but a
girl's best friend is still a nearsighted man.

YOKO ONO

Day 329

. . . .

Unexpected Guests

Remember that old expression:
"Back door guests are best?" It's true,
even when they're unexpected or uninvited.
Some friends are so dear that you swing
wide your door, no matter when they
arrive. Invitation? Who needs one!
C'mon over!

Day 330

. . . .

The Best Way to Take Off Weight

I have a great diet. You're allowed to eat anything you want, but you must eat it with naked fat people.

ED BLUESTONE

Day 331

A Picnic in the Park

Don't you love picnics? (Minus the ants, of course.) There's something kind of cheesy, but fun, about taking your food outdoors, spreading a quilt under a shade tree, and eating with nature as your backdrop. Add friends and family, and you've got a recipe for a fabulous afternoon!

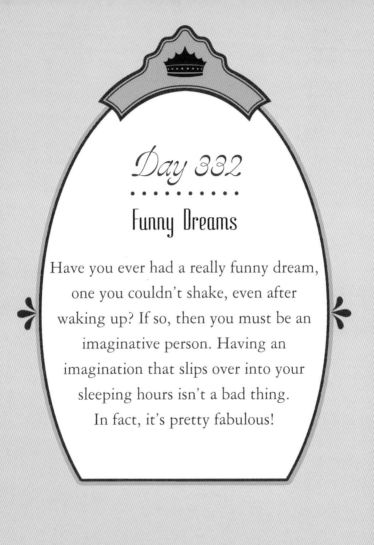

Day 332

. . . .

Funny Dreams

Have you ever had a really funny dream, one you couldn't shake, even after waking up? If so, then you must be an imaginative person. Having an imagination that slips over into your sleeping hours isn't a bad thing. In fact, it's pretty fabulous!

Day 333
· · · · · · · · · · · ·
Diva Envy

A diva is someone who pretends to know
who she is and looks fabulous doing it.

JENIFER LEWIS

Day 334

· · · · · · · · · ·

Perseverance

Having a stick-to-it attitude is so
important for women, no matter the
situation. There's something about that
"I'm not giving up, no matter what!"
attitude that makes people sit up and take
notice. Don't give up. Don't give in. . .
no matter what you're facing.
Stand strong. Persevere.

Day 335
. . . .
Laughter and Tears

Laugh and the world laughs with you.
Cry and you cry with your girlfriends.

LAURIE KUSLANSKY

Day 336

Digital Picture Frames

Don't you love those great digital picture frames? They're fabulous, aren't they? They're also a great way to keep the faces of those you love in front of you at all times.

Day 337

· · · · · · · · · · ·

Knowing Your Limits

Have enough sense to know,
ahead of time, when your skills will not
extend to wallpapering.

MARILYN VOS SAVANT

Day 338

. . . .

Marathon Shopper

Don't you love those marathon shopping days? You spend hours and hours searching for just the right item. Marathon shopping kills two birds with one stone: you get everything done in a day, and you get a lot of exercise, too. Only one thing makes a marathon shopping day better. . . going with a friend.

Day 339
. . . .
Comfort Food

I love to cook comfort food. I'll make fish
and vegetables or meat and vegetables and
potatoes or rice. The ritual of it is fun for
me, and the creativity of it.

REESE WITHERSPOON

Day 340

Breakfast in Bed

Having breakfast served to you in bed is such a luxury, high on a woman's "fabulosity" list! There's something about reclining under the covers with a tray of goodies that makes you feel cozy. Toast, tea, jam, omelet, bacon, eggs. . .you name it, it's yummier in bed!

Day 341

Babies

A baby will make love stronger,
days shorter, nights longer, bankroll
smaller, home happier, clothes shabbier,
the past forgotten, and the future
worth living for.

UNKNOWN

Day 342

· · · · · · · · · · ·

A Puppy's Kisses

Not everyone is infatuated with dogs, but for those who are, there's nothing sweeter than a puppy's kisses. With one slobbery kiss, he convinces you that you're the greatest human being in the world.

Day 343
· · · · · · · · · · ·
Being the Normal One in the Family

Are you the normal one in your family?
When others around you are going a little
crazy, do you manage to keep your sanity?
There's something to be said for being
the only sane one in the bunch!
Why not celebrate that fact?

Day 344

. . . .

Kid-Friendly Organizations

All around the world, children are in need. They need clean water, proper health care, food, school supplies, and someone to care. We can show our love through great organizations that reach out to these children and meet their needs in a tangible way. The ability to link arms by sending a monthly check is truly fabulous!

Day 345

. . . .

Several Days at Once

I try to take one day at a time,
but sometimes several days
attack me at once.

JENNIFER UNLIMITED

Day 346

. . . .

Beautiful and Splendid Things

Life has loveliness to sell, all beautiful and
splendid things, blue waves whitened on
a cliff, soaring fire that sways and sings,
and children's faces looking up,
holding wonder like a cup.

SARA TEASDALE

Day 347

· · · · · · · · · · ·

A Level Playing Field

Women today don't always have to scratch
their way to the top, as in generations
before. That said, they do know the benefit
of coming into a job, political situation,
or organization on a level playing field.
When others play fair, we're able to
perform at the top of our game.

Day 348

. . . .

Zest!

Zest is the secret of all beauty.
There is no beauty that is
attractive without zest.

CHRISTIAN DIOR

Day 349

Family Ties

You can travel the world over. . .
make hundreds of friends. You can work
alongside some of the best people in your
industry. You can go to school with some
really amazing people. But in the end,
family ties are still the strongest.
They bind us together and make us strong.

Day 350

· · · · · · · · · · ·

Fashion Sense

I base most of my fashion
sense on what doesn't itch.

GILDA RADNER

Day 351
. . . .
Big-Hearted People

Don't you love generous, big-hearted
people? They're always looking out for the
other guy, ready to meet needs or extend
a hand of generosity. Best of all,
big-hearted folks don't make a show of
their giving. They're simply there at the
right moment, ready to help.

Day 352

• • • • • • • • • • •

Kind and Understanding

I want a man who's kind and
understanding. Is that too much to
ask of a millionaire?

ZSA ZSA GABOR

Day 353
· · · · · · · · · · ·
Near Misses

Accidents that "almost" happened,
but didn't. Mortgage payments that
"almost" didn't get paid, but did.
These near misses might seem frightening
in the moment, but when you look back at
how you were spared, how things worked
out in the end, you have to admit,
near misses are pretty fabulous!

Day 354
. . . .
The Little Black Dress

Admit it. . .every woman loves her little
black dress. It's the perfect thing to pull
out of the closet for special events, and you
can dress it up or dress it down depending
on the occasion. And there's nothing
more fun than hearing, "Girl, you look
fabulous!" when you're wearing it!

Day 355
∙ ∙ ∙ ∙ ∙ ∙ ∙ ∙ ∙ ∙

Ask a Woman

In politics, if you
want anything said,
ask a man. If you
want anything done,
ask a woman.

MARGARET THATCHER

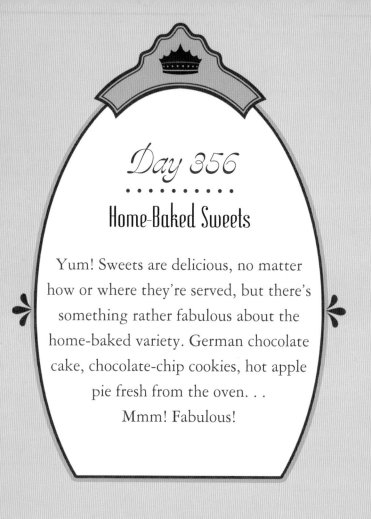

Day 356

· · · · · · · · · · ·

Home-Baked Sweets

Yum! Sweets are delicious, no matter
how or where they're served, but there's
something rather fabulous about the
home-baked variety. German chocolate
cake, chocolate-chip cookies, hot apple
pie fresh from the oven. . .

Mmm! Fabulous!

Day 357

· · · · · · · · · · ·

Dance Class

If you've ever taken a dance class—
ballroom dancing, line dancing, swing,
or otherwise—you know that hitting the
dance floor can be a great stress reliever.
It also makes you feel young! As you
two-step your way across the floor, you feel
like a kid again! Fabulous!

Day 358

· · · · · · · · · ·

Naming Things (and People)

Women give things fabulous little names.
We call a get-together a "snack 'n' yak."
We label our party foods with cute names,
give our kids nicknames, and call others,
"hon," "sweetie," or "cupcake" just for fun.
We're all about naming—and renaming—
things and people. What fun!

Day 359

· · · · · · · · · · ·

A Great Hand Lotion

Those with dry skin really appreciate a
great hand lotion. In the middle of winter,
when the cold weather is taking its toll,
hands can get dry and cracked. A fabulous
lotion feels like a trip to the spa. Add a
dollop to your palm, then "lotion up"
those dry hands, elbows, and heels!

Day 360
· · · · · · · · · · ·
Enjoy the Ride!

Chocolate doesn't make the world
go around. . .but it certainly
makes the ride worthwhile!

UNKNOWN

Day 361

. . . .

A Friend Who Prays

When you're down and need someone to
turn to, there nothing better than knowing
you've got a friend who will pray for you.
She lifts up your needs and won't stop until
your situation improves. There's only one
thing better than having a praying friend,
and that's being one!

Day 362
. . . .
Living Long. . .and Wide

I don't want to get to the end of my life
and find that I lived just the length of it.
I want to have lived the width of it as well.

DIANE ACKERMAN

Day 363
. . . .
Being in Love

I love you not only for what you are,
but for what I am when I am with you.
I love you not only for what you are
making of me. I love you for the part of
me that you bring out.

Roy Croft

Day 364

Holidays with Friends and Family

How fabulous, to spend holidays
surrounded by those we love.
Family members—young and old—
friends, neighbors. What joy to share
special days with those who are
most special to us.

Day 365

. . . .

The Great Question. . .

Despite my thirty years of research into
the feminine soul, I have not yet been able
to answer the great question that has never
been answered: What does a woman want?

SIGMUND FREUD

Notes

....
....
....
....
....
....
....
....
....
....
....
....
....
....
....
....
....
....
....
....
....
....
....

Notes

Notes

. . . .
. . . .
. . . .
. . . .
. . . .
. . . .
. . . .
. . . .
. . . .
. . . .
. . . .
. . . .
. . . .
. . . .
. . . .
. . . .
. . . .
. . . .
. . . .
. . . .
. . . .
. . . .

Notes

Notes

Notes

. . . .
. . . .
. . . .
. . . .
. . . .
. . . .
. . . .
. . . .
. . . .
. . . .
. . . .
. . . .
. . . .
. . . .
. . . .
. . . .
. . . .
. . . .
. . . .
. . . .
. . . .
. . . .
. . . .
. . . .

Notes

....
....
....
....
....
....
....
....
....
....
....
....
....
....
....
....
....
....
....
....
....
....

Notes

....
....
....
....
....
....
....
....
....
....
....
....
....
....
....
....
....
....
....
....
....
....
....
....

Notes

Notes

Notes

Notes

Notes

....
....
....
....
....
....
....
....
....
....
....
....
....
....
....
....
....
....
....
....

Notes

. . . .
. . . .
. . . .
. . . .
. . . .
. . . .
. . . .
. . . .
. . . .
. . . .
. . . .
. . . .
. . . .
. . . .
. . . .
. . . .
. . . .
. . . .
. . . .
. . . .
. . . .
. . . .